PHONIC CROSSWORDS

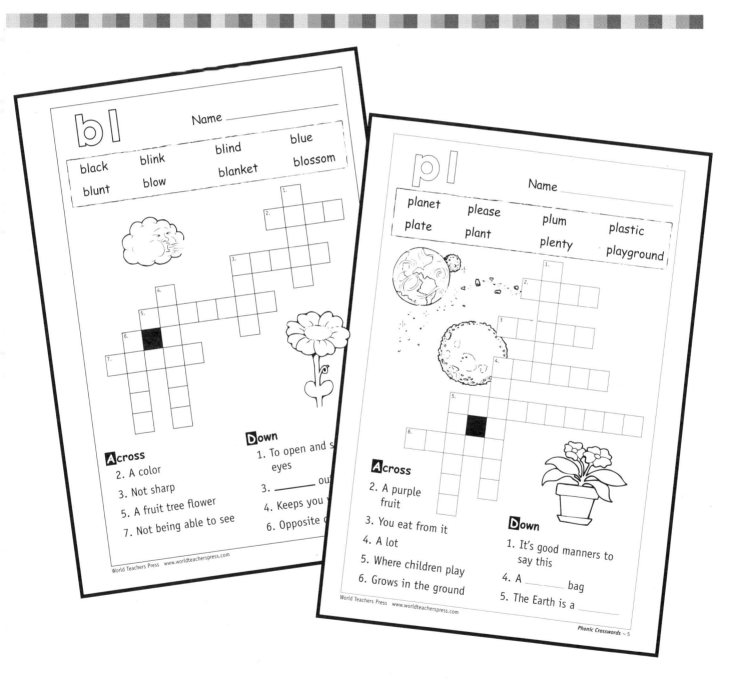

bl

Name _____

black   blink   blind   blue
blunt   blow   blanket   blossom

Across
2. A color
3. Not sharp
5. A fruit tree flower
7. Not being able to see

Down
1. To open and s... eyes
3. _____ ou...
4. Keeps you ...
6. Opposite o...

pl

Name _____

planet   please   plum   plastic
plate   plant   plenty   playground

Across
2. A purple fruit
3. You eat from it
4. A lot
5. Where children play
6. Grows in the ground

Down
1. It's good manners to say this
4. A _____ bag
5. The Earth is a _____

by Jenny Preston

Published with the permission of R.I.C. Publications Pty. Ltd.

First published by R.I.C. Publications Pty. Ltd., Perth, Western Australia. Revised by Didax Educational Resources.

Printed in the United States of America.

Order Number 2-5202
ISBN 1-58324-141-8

A B C D E F 06 05 04 03 02

Educational Resources
395 Main Street
Rowley, MA 01969
www.worldteacherspress.com

Foreword

Phonic Crosswords is designed as a supplement and reinforcement resource to the teaching of phonics. The book covers consonant blends and digraphs, vowel digraphs, vowel consonant blends and digraphs, trigraphs and silent letters.

The crosswords are suitable for use with individual students, small groups, or as a whole-class activity. The size of the crossword squares has been designed to accomodate large printing and the artwork used reflects the content of each page.

All words to be used are given at the top of each page, however if the teacher desires the words can covered before photocopying.

Answers are included.

Contents

	Page		Page		Page		Page
bl	5	tw	27	ar	49	air	71
cl	6	scr	28	er	50	all	72
fl	7	spl, spr	29	ir	51	ear	73
gl	8	str	30	or	52	our	74
pl	9	ing	31	ur	53	wor	75
sl	10	ung, ang	32	ay	54	w	76
br	11	ank	33	ey	55	b	77
cr	12	ink	34	le	56	k	78
dr	13	ill, ell	35	ow	57	a	79
fr	14	oll, ull	36	oy	58	o	80
gr	15	old	37	a-e	59	o	81
pr	16	squ	38	ee	60	ce, cy	82
tr	17	ch	39	ie	61	ice, ace	83
sc	18	sh	40	i-e	62	ge, gi	84
sk	19	th	41	o-e	63		
sn	20	wh	42	u-e	64	Answers... 85 – 88	
sm	21	ck	43	oa	65		
sp	22	nch	44	oi	66		
st	23	tch	45	oo	67		
sw	24	thr	46	ou	68		
lt, mp	25	qu	47	ai	69		
nt, nd	26	wa	48	ea	70		

Teacher's Notes

Phonic Crosswords are suitable for use with individual students, small groups, or as a whole-class activity.

The phonic sound covered is outlined for students to color and focus on.

The artwork reflects part of the content of the page.

List of words to be used to complete the crosswords. Teachers may cover these before photocopying to increase the level of difficulty for some students.

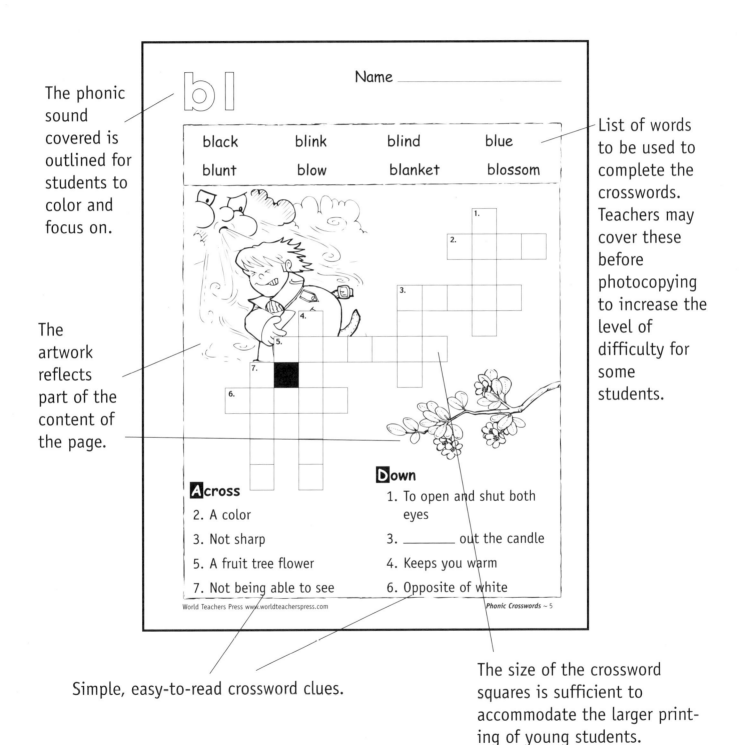

bl

Name _____

black   blink   blind   blue

blunt   blow   blanket   blossom

Across

2. A color

3. Not sharp

5. A fruit tree flower

7. Not being able to see

Down

1. To open and shut both eyes

3. _____ out the candle

4. Keeps you warm

6. Opposite of white

World Teachers Press www.worldteacherspress.com

Phonic Crosswords ~ 5

Simple, easy-to-read crossword clues.

The size of the crossword squares is sufficient to accommodate the larger printing of young students.

Answers are provided on pages 85 – 88.

Name _____

| black | blink | blind | blue |
| blunt | blow | blanket | blossom |

Across

2. A color

3. Not sharp

5. A fruit tree flower

7. Not being able to see

Down

1. To open and shut both eyes

3. _____ out the candle

4. Keeps you warm

6. Opposite of white

| class | clown | close | cloud |
| clear | cluck | clock | clever |

Across

3. A _____ of children

5. Very smart

6. Keeps the time

8. Seen in the sky

Down

1. Opposite of far

2. Glass is _____

4. The call of a chicken

7. A funny person

fl

Name _____

| flock | float | flood | flower |
| flour | flash | floor | flounder |

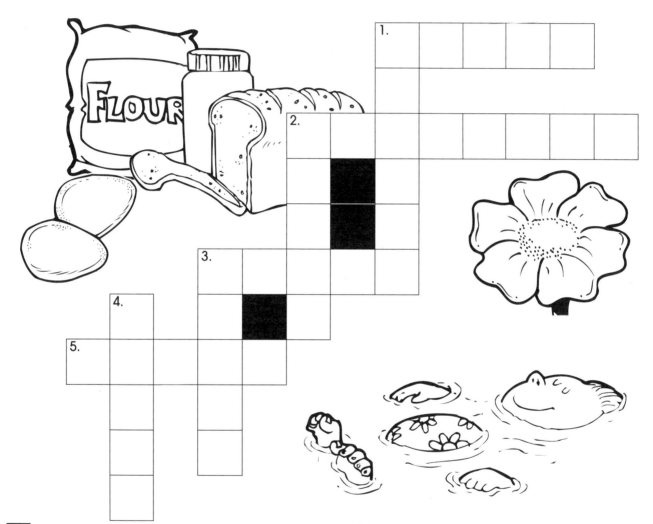

Across

1. A group of sheep
2. A fish
3. Used to make bread
5. Opposite of sink

Down

1. Found on a plant
2. You walk on it
3. A sudden bright light
4. To wash over with water

Name _____

glove   glide   glass   gleam

glare   glue   globe   glad

Across

2. Happy

3. Sticks things together

5. To shine

7. To fly

Down

1. You wear this on your hand

3. You drink out of one

4. An angry look

6. A model of the Earth

| planet | please | plum | plastic |
| plate | plant | plenty | playground |

Across

2. A purple fruit

3. You eat from it

4. A lot

5. Where children play

6. Grows in the ground

Down

1. It's good manners to say this

4. A _____ bag

5. The Earth is a _____

sl

Name _____

| sleeve | slave | slim | slam |
| sleep | sling | slow | slipper |

Across

1. Opposite of fast
2. To throw
4. Worn on the foot
5. What you do at night

Down

1. Opposite of fat
2. Part of a shirt
3. Work very hard
5. To shut hard

World Teachers Press® www.worldteacherspress.com

br

Name _____

brave	bread	brush	bright
breeze	break	brown	branch

Across

3. Not easily frightened
5. Opposite of dull
7. A color
8. To come apart

Down

1. You eat it
2. _____ your teeth
3. Part of a tree
6. Similar to wind

cr

| crayon | crow | crash | creak |
| crawl | cream | creek | crab |

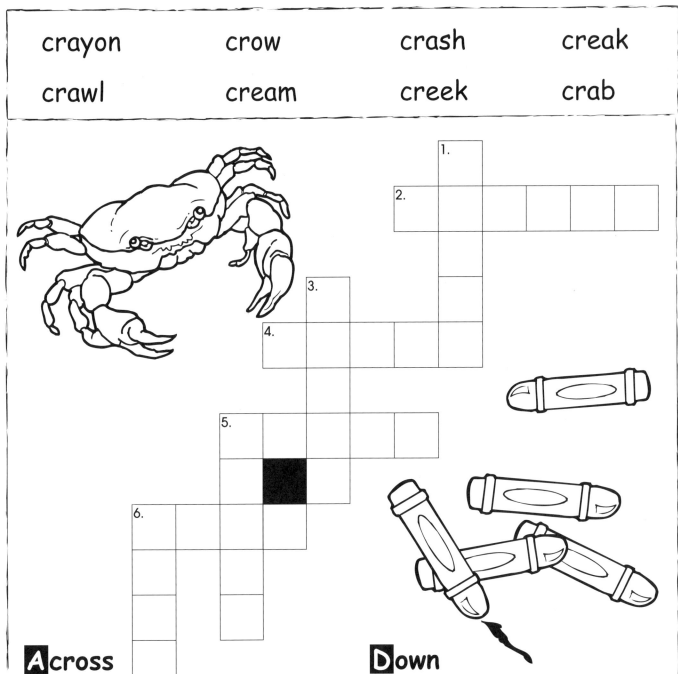

Across

2. You draw with it

4. A sound made by a door

5. A baby does this

6. A small sea animal

Down

1. A small stream

3. Comes from milk

5. To smash together

6. A black bird

dr

Name _____

dress	drag	draw	drink
dream	drop	drive	dragon

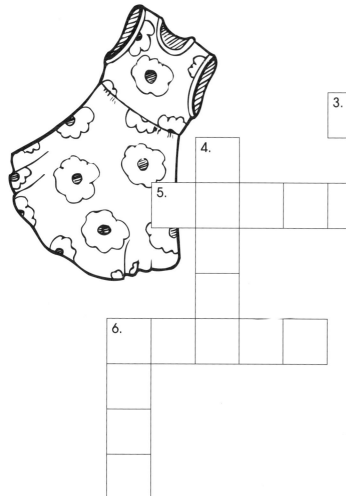

Across

1. _____ a picture
3. You do it in your sleep
5. It breathes fire
6. That is a pretty _____

Down

1. To pull along
2. You _____ water
4. You _____ a car
6. To let fall

fr

Name _____

frost	fresh	frog	frown
fruit	front	fried	fridge

Across

1. A small jumping animal
2. Like ice
4. Keeps food cold
6. Opposite of back

Down

1. An unhappy look
2. Opposite of stale
3. You eat it
5. Cooked in a pan

World Teachers Press® www.worldteacherspress.com

gr

| grub | growl | green | ground |
| grab | grow | grass | grape |

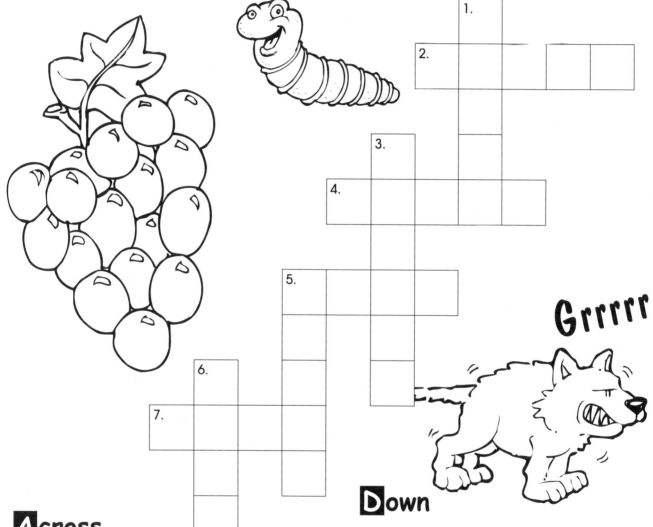

Grrrrr

Across

2. Grows in the yard

4. A color

5. Young insect

7. To get bigger

Down

1. A small fruit

3. Plants grow in the _____

5. To make an angry sound

6. To take something

Name _____

price	pretty	present	protect
prey	press	prize	sprint

Across

2. A hunted animal

3. To push down

6. To keep safe

7. What something costs

Down

1. You win a _____

3. Good or nice looking

4. To race at top speed

5. A birthday _____

   World Teachers Press® www.worldteacherspress.com

tr

Name _____

| trunk | trot | train | tray |
| truck | trick | trumpet | trouble |

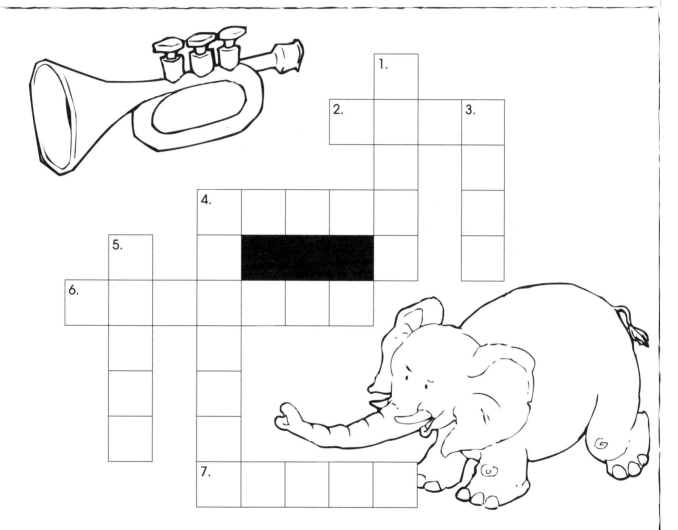

Across

2. A slow run

4. Runs on rails

6. A problem

7. A magic _____

Down

1. An elephant has one

3. Used to carry food

4. A musical instrument

5. A dump _____

SC

Name _____

scar   scale   scratch   scream

score   screen   escape   scowl

Across

2. To look angry

3. A TV _____

6. Points in a game

7. Mark left by a burn

Down

1. Found on a fish

3. You _____ an itch

4. To get away

5. A frightened call

sk

 Name _____

skunk	skull	skip	sketch
skate	skill	skirt	skeleton

Across

2. _____ board

3. Part of a dress

5. The bones of an animal

7. Ability to be good at something

Down

1. A small furry animal

3. To draw

4. The head bones

6. To jump over a rope

snake	snow	snatch	snack
snail	snap	sniff	sneeze

ah-choo !

1.

2.

3.

4.

5.

6.

Across

1. Cold and white

2. To break

4. Happens during a cold

5. To smell something

6. A small meal

Down

1. A dangerous animal

3. An animal with a shell

5. To grab something

 World Teachers Press® www.worldteacherspress.com

| smooth | small | smile | smack |
| smell | smart | smoke | smash |

Across

1. The nose does it
2. Clever
4. Having no bumps
6. To make a happy face
7. Caused by fire

Down

1. Break into pieces
3. Tiny
5. To hit sharply

sp

Name _____

spin	spine	speed	special
wasp	spill	sprint	sport

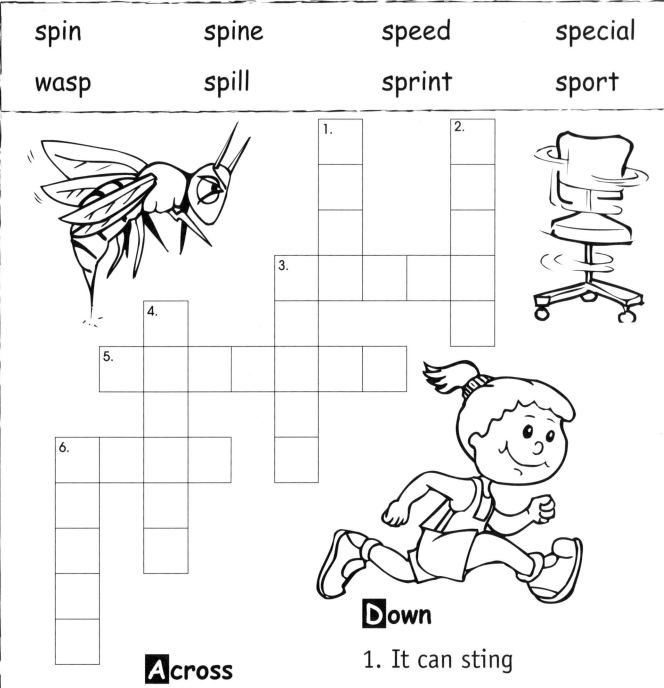

Across

3. Your backbone

5. New year is a _____ time of year

6. To turn around quickly

Down

1. It can sting

2. To drive too fast

3. To tip over

4. A short, fast run

6. Football is a _____

World Teachers Press® www.worldteacherspress.com

Name _____

nest   fast   star   first

step   start   gust   stick

Across

2. A bird _____

4. Seen in the night sky

5. Opposite of last

7. Very quick

Down

1. A _____ of wind

3. A piece of wood

6. Same as begin

8. Watch your _____

Name _____

| swamp | swap | sweet | sweep |
| swarm | swan | swing | swift |

1.

2.

3.

4.

5.

6.

7.

Across

2. Many insects

3. To trade something

5. To clean with a broom

7. Very quick

Down

1. A white bird

2. A wet-land

4. Like sugar

6. Move backwards and forwards

Name _____

| felt | melt | belt | built |
| jump | lamp | pump | stamp |

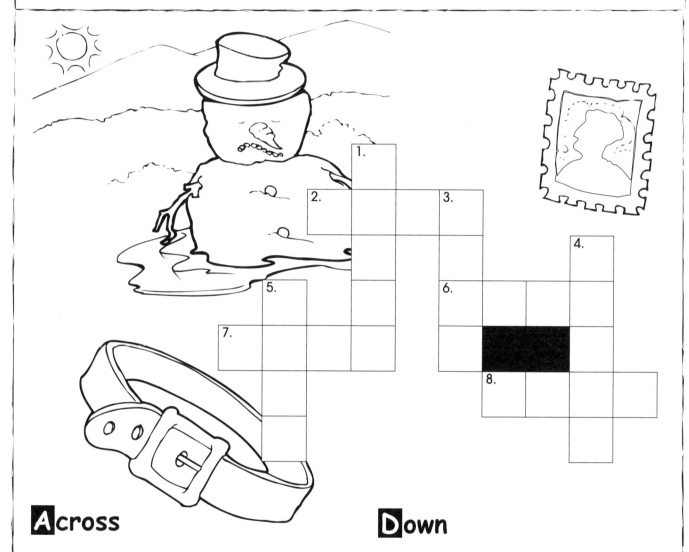

Across

2. To leap over something

6. Ice can _____ into water

7. A car seat_____

8. Gives off light

Down

1. The house that Jack _____

3. You _____ up a tire

4. Put on a letter

5. It _____ smooth

nt, nd

Name _____

| mend | hand | bend | friend |
| cent | tent | paint | ant |

Across

4. A small insect

5. Used when camping

7. To curve

8. It has five fingers

Down

1. 100 of these make a dollar

2. To _____ a picture

3. Someone that helps you

6. To fix

World Teachers Press® www.worldteacherspress.com

tw

Name _____

twine	twirl	tweet	twinkle
twin	twig	twelve	twist

Across

2. To spin

4. A bird noise

7. An exact copy

8. The number after eleven

Down

1. Another word for string

3. To shine or gleam

5. To wind together

6. A small branch

Name _____

scrape   screen   scream   scribble

scrub   scrap   scruffy   screech

1.

2.

3.

4.

5.

Across

1. A television _____

2. To clean

4. A loud cry

5. Untidy writing

Down

1. To smooth by rubbing

3. A frightened shout

4. Untidy looking

5. A small piece of food

World Teachers Press® www.worldteacherspress.com

Name _____

| split | splint | splinter | splash |
| spray | spring | spread | sprinkle |

Across

2. To wet with water

5. Light rain

7. A mist of water

8. A coil of wire

Down

1. Helps a broken bone

3. A _____ of wood

4. To cover with a thin layer

6. To cut or chop

str

Name _____

Across

2. A type of road

3. Opposite of weak

4. Different or weird

5. A small river

Down

1. Dried grass

2. A kite _____

3. Decoration

4. A band of color

ing

Name _____

swing   wing   sting   singing

spring   fling   ring   string

Across

3. A season

5. _____ a song

7. Something you put on a finger

Down

1. To throw

2. A bee can _____

3. Used to tie knots

4. Found in a playground

6. Part of a bird

ung, ang

| rung | fang | bang | rang |
| sang | stung | clang | hunger |

Across

3. An empty feeling

6. They _____ a song

7. The noise a gun makes

8. A step on a ladder

Down

1. Loud ringing noise

2. A bee _____ me

4. The telephone _____

5. A snake's tooth

| bank | tank | crank | sank |
| thank | drank | spank | plank |

1.

2.

3.

4.

5.

6.

7.

Across

3. Used to start old cars

5. A "grateful" word

6. To hit for punishment

7. The gas _____ was full

Down

1. A place to keep money

2. She _____ the water

4. A long piece of wood

6. The boat _____

ink

Name _____

pink	think	sink	twinkle
shrink	drink	blink	rink

Across

1. A place to wash dishes
2. A place to ice skate
4. " _____ _____ little star"
5. You do it with your eyes
6. A color

Down

1. To get smaller
3. You _____ water
4. Happens in your head

    World Teachers Press® www.worldteacherspress.com

ill, ell

sell	fell	bell	shell
mill	fill	hill	still

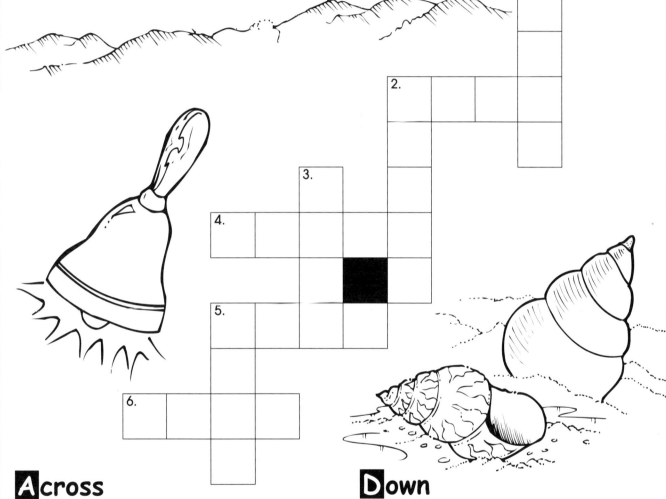

Across

2. Opposite of buy

4. Part of an animal

5. He _____ off his bike

6. Where flour is made

Down

1. You walk up a

   _____

2. Not moving

3. Made from metal

5. _____ the bucket

oll, ull

gull	pull	dull	full
doll	collar	jolly	dollar

Across

3. Part of a shirt

5. The bin was _____

7. Not shiny

8. A toy

Down

1. Happy

2. 100 cents make a _____

4. A seabird

6. Opposite of push

Name _____

| sold | bold | old | fold |
| hold | cold | gold | told |

Across

2. Opposite of young

4. Showing no fear

6. A color

8. Opposite of hot

Down

1. _____ the paper in half

3. Opposite of bought

5. She _____ the truth

7. _____ hands

squ

Name _____

| squirt | squid | squint | squirrel |
| squeal | squeeze | squash | squelch |

Across

2. Eyes half closed

3. A cry of pain

4. Splashing sound

5. To spray water

Down

1. To flatten or crush

3. A small furry animal

4. To press hard

5. A sea animal

ch

Name _____

| chin | rich | child | chop |
| chick | cheer | chest | cheese |

Across

1. A baby chicken

3. Made from milk

4. Opposite of poor

6. Opposite of adult

Down

1. A happy shout

2. Treasure is kept in a

   _____

5. Part of the face

6. To cut by hitting

sh

finish	shoe	fish	ship
shop	wish	shut	brush

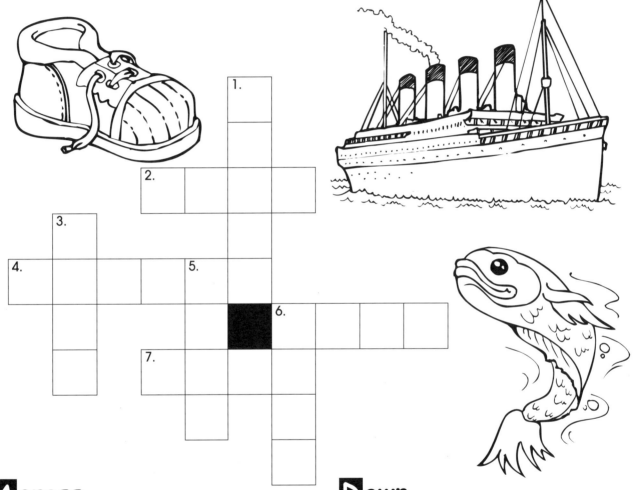

Across

2. To close

4. To end

6. You put it on your foot

7. Close your eyes and make a _____

Down

1. You _____ your hair

3. A water creature

5. It floats on water

6. A place that sells things

th

| thin | three | thank | thirteen |
| them | moth | thorn | thing |

Across

1. It is sharp
2. An "unlucky" number
4. _____ you
5. Ask _____, not me

Down

1. Some_____
2. Opposite of thick
3. A small number
6. An insect

Name _____

| whip | where | wheel | whisper |
| white | wheat | why | whale |

Across

1. A word that is a question

3. You grow it

5. A quiet talk

6. Sounds the same as "wear"

Down

1. A large ocean creature

2. Opposite of black

4. A round object

6. Something you hit with

World Teachers Press® www.worldteacherspress.com

ck

Name _____

| duck | black | sock | clock |
| truck | trick | block | sick |

Across

2. To feel ill
4. To fool
6. Keeps time
7. Very dark

Down

1. A waterbird
2. Worn on the foot
3. A large vehicle
5. A _____ of wood

nch

finch	ranch	bench	lunch
bunch	punch	branch	crunch

Across

3. A place to keep cattle

5. A _____ of grapes

8. The midday meal

Down

1. A small bird

2. Part of a tree

4. To hit with the fist

6. To crush noisily

7. A work_____

tch

Name _____

| witch | hutch | catch | match |
| stitch | switch | itch | scratch |

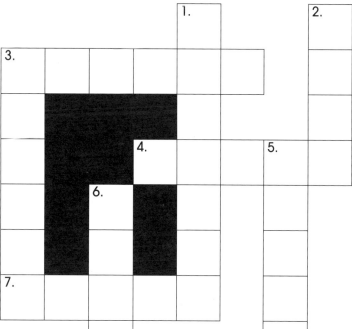

Across

3. A light _____

4. It can start fires

7. A type of animal cage

Down

1. A type of cut

2. You scratch an

   _____

3. Part of sewing

5. To _____ a ball

6. Rides a broomstick

thr

thrill	throne	three	thrush
throat	thrash	throw	through

3

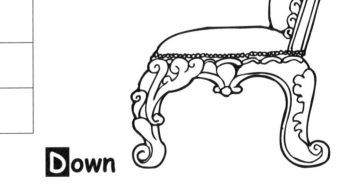

Across

1. Part of the neck

3. A type of bird

4. Caused by excitement

5. She walked _____ the door

Down

1. To beat easily

2. After two

4. A king or queen's chair

5. You _____ a ball

Name _____

quilt	quiet	queen	quick
queer	quite	quack	question

Across

3. It's _____ cloudy

5. A duck call

6. Opposite of answer

Down

1. Strange

2. Fast

4. Opposite of king

5. No sound

6. A blanket

wa

Name _____

wasp	watch	wattle	waddle
wash	wander	wallet	wallaby

Across

2. An Australian animal
4. To walk around
5. Holds money
6. _____ your hands

Down

1. An insect that stings
2. A duck's walk
3. An Australian plant
5. _____ out!

   World Teachers Press® www.worldteacherspress.com

ar

Name _____

march	tart	sharp	farm
shark	park	mark	start

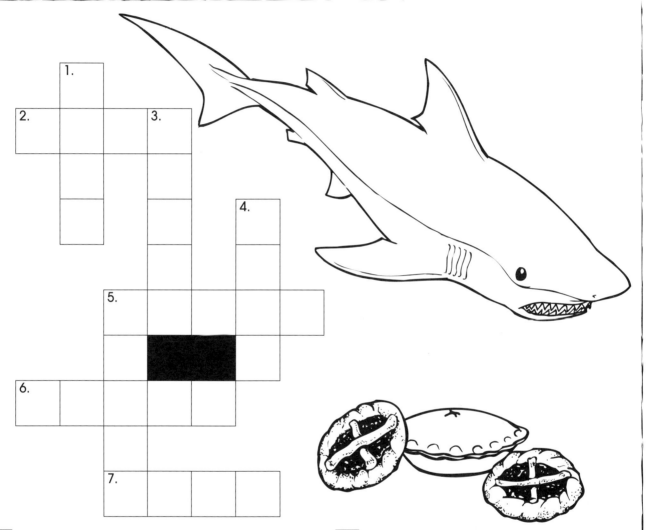

Across

2. A place for animals
5. A knife is _____
6. Lives in the ocean
7. A small pie

Down

1. A place for trees
3. Soldiers _____
4. A spot
5. Same as "begin"

er

Name _____

| river | fern | ladder | clever |
| gather | mother | father | jumper |

Across

3. To collect together

4. _____ and father

6. Very smart

8. A type of plant

Down

1. _____ and mother

2. Sleeveless dress

5. Large water stream

7. You climb it

World Teachers Press® www.worldteacherspress.com

ir

Name _____

first	girl	shirt	bird
third	skirt	thirst	stir

Across

2. Opposite of boy

4. Girl's clothes

5. Water will help this

7. A flying animal

8. Mix with a spoon

Down

1. Opposite of last

3. Comes after second

6. A _____ and tie

or

Name _____

| porch | torch | more | horse |
| cork | fork | born | thorn |

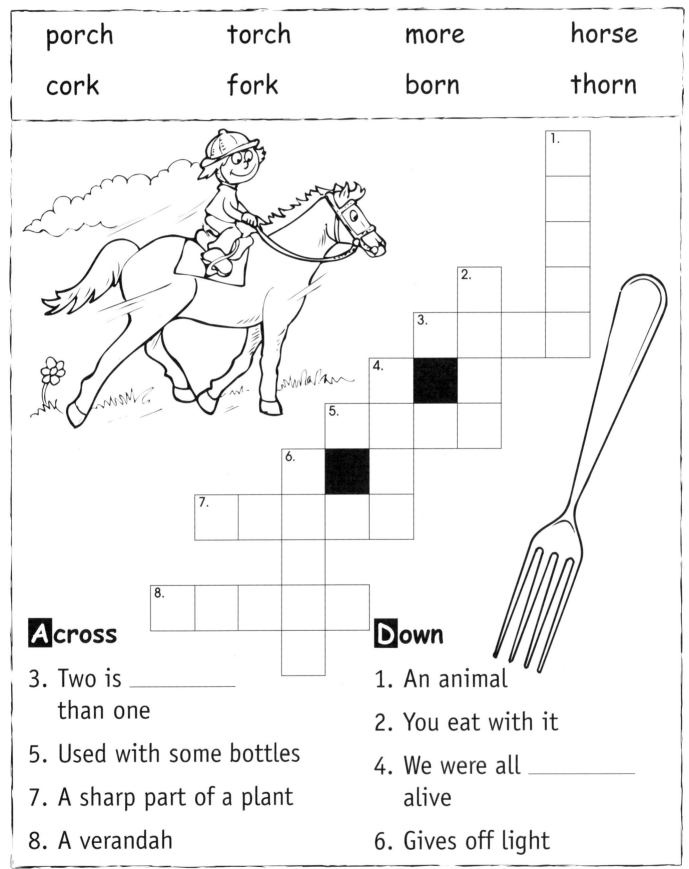

Across

3. Two is _____ than one

5. Used with some bottles

7. A sharp part of a plant

8. A verandah

Down

1. An animal

2. You eat with it

4. We were all _____ alive

6. Gives off light

World Teachers Press® www.worldteacherspress.com

Name _____

| curl | turnip | lurch | turtle |
| further | burn | burst | Saturday |

Across

2. To break

6. You can see _____ on a clear day

8. A ring of hair

Down

1. Fire can _____ you

3. A day of the week

4. To stagger

5. A vegetable

7. Has a hard shell

Name _____

play   hay   clay   bay

tray   stay   away   sway

Across

2. Dry grass

5. Used to carry food

7. I like to _____ music

8. Move from side to side

Down

1. A body of water

3. Put _____ your toys

4. To remain behind

6. A type of earth or mud

   World Teachers Press® www.worldteacherspress.com

jockey	turkey	donkey	monkey
parsley	chimney	key	trolley

Across

3. Herb used in cooking

4. Smoke goes up it

7. Similar to a horse

8. A large bird

Down

1. Helps carry heavy things

2. Unlocks and locks doors

5. Climbs trees

6. Rides horses

| rifle | puddle | needle | beetle |
| turtle | poodle | eagle | jungle |

Across

2. A place full of trees

3. A bird

5. A type of dog

6. An ocean creature

8. An insect

Down

1. Has a very sharp point

4. A _____ of water

7. Shoots a bullet

World Teachers Press® www.worldteacherspress.com

OW

Name _____

| shadow | narrow | hollow | slow |
| crow | grow | know | row |

Across

3. Not wide

5. Opposite of fast

6. To get bigger

7. To _____ a boat

8. To learn something

Down

1. Give shade

2. Empty inside

4. A bird

oy

Name _____

| joy | boy | annoy | destroy |
| enjoy | toy | ahoy | oyster |

1.

2.

3. 4. 5. 6.

7.

Across

2. Sailor's call

3. To break

7. Girl, woman; _____, man

Down

1. Great happiness

2. To pester someone

4. To have a good time

5. Something to play with

6. A shellfish

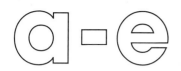

Name _____

| lake | grape | spade | plane |
| whale | snake | game | cake |

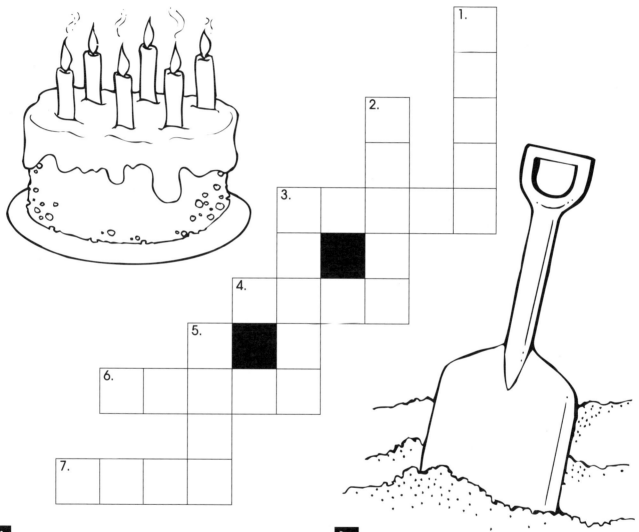

Across

3. A garden tool
4. A body of water
6. A large ocean animal
7. Baked in an oven

Down

1. It can fly
2. A fruit
3. Has no legs
5. Chess is a _____

ee

Name _____

| sneeze | tree | cheese | thirteen |
| cheep | free | see | freeze |

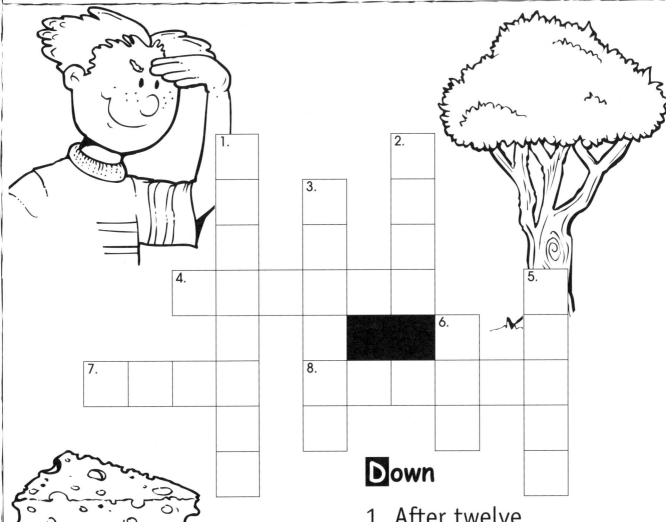

Across

4. To make very cold

7. Costing nothing

8. Happens during a cold

Down

1. After twelve

2. Wood comes from this

3. Made from milk

5. A bird noise

6. I can _____ with my eyes

World Teachers Press® www.worldteacherspress.com

ie

Name _____

| lied | tie | died | cried |
| pie | die | tied | fried |

Across

2. To stop living

4. To be cooked in oil

5. She _____ her shoelaces

6. An apple _____

Down

1. The boy _____ to me

2. Without water, the plant _____

3. She _____ after being burnt

5. Worn around the neck

i-e

Name _____

smile	time	pipe	dive
slide	hide	hive	like

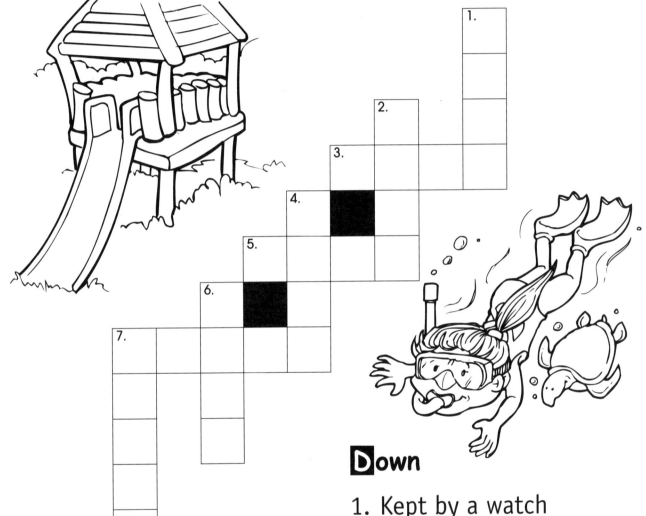

Across

3. A bee's home

5. _____ and seek

7. Found in the playground

Down

1. Kept by a watch

2. I _____ ice cream

4. I like to _____ into water

6. A drain _____

7. Make a happy face

   World Teachers Press® www.worldteacherspress.com

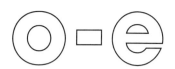

Name _____

home   rope   rode   drove

stone   throne   slope   stove

Across

1. Used to tie up

3. Something very hard

6. A king's chair

7. You live in it

Down

1. They _____ their bikes

2. A ski _____

4. Used for cooking

5. We _____ to the store

u-e

prune	June	mute	pollute
rude	flute	ruler	salute

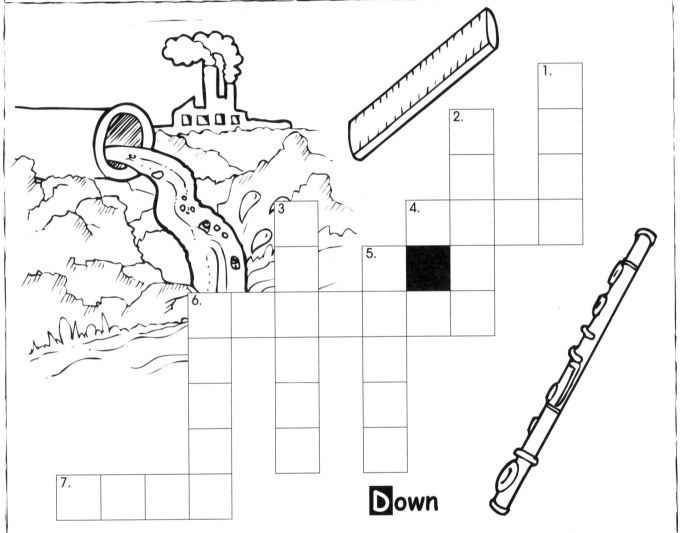

Across

4. Bad mannered

6. To make dirty

7. A month of the year

Down

1. Making no sound

2. A musical instrument

3. What soldiers do

5. Helps draw lines

6. A dried plum

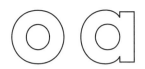

Name _____

coach   croak   goat   float

coat   cloak   boat   soak

Across

3. An animal

4. You wear it

5. Pulled by horses

7. Rest in water

Down

1. It floats on water

2. Opposite of sink

4. The sound a frog makes

6. Like a coat

Name _____

oil   coil   soil   spoil

coin   boil   moist   noise

Across

2. A form of money

5. Another word for damp

6. Used in cars

8. To ruin

Down

1. A very painful sore

3. A loud _____

4. To curl up

7. You grow plants on it

Name _____

room   broom   droop   tooth

spoon   boot   moon   food

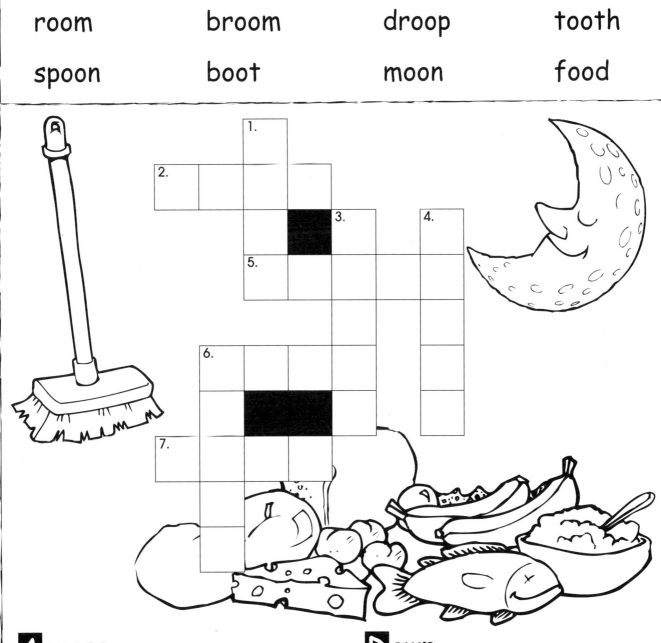

Across

2. A place in the home
5. To bend over
6. You put it on your foot
7. Seen mostly at night

Down

1. You eat it
3. Found in your mouth
4. You eat with it
6. Used for sweeping

ou

Name _____

cloud   mouse   house   found

loud   couch   round   sound

Across

2. A place to sit

4. Opposite of lost

6. A small animal

8. Seen in the sky

Down

1. Like a circle

3. You live in one

5. A loud _____

7. A _____ noise

World Teachers Press® www.worldteacherspress.com

Name _____

rain   mail   paint   chain

nail   train   stain   sail

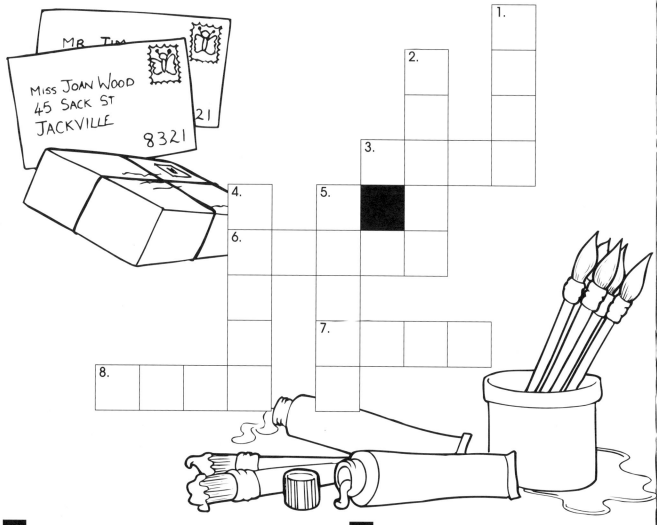

Across

3. You read this

6. Runs on rails

7. Made from steel

8. Comes from the sky

Down

1. Part of a ship

2. Found on a bike

4. A dirty mark

5. Can be colored

Name _____

peach	seat	sea	clean
steam	speak	meat	seam

Across

2. A join in a dress

5. Very hot

6. A place for boats

7. You wash to keep _____

Down

1. You can rest in one

3. You cook it

4. A fruit

5. _____ quietly

World Teachers Press® www.worldteacherspress.com

Name _____

| fair | dairy | chair | stair |
| pair | fairy | hair | airplane |

1.
2.
3.
4.
5.
6.
7.

Across

3. Found on your head

5. A machine that can fly

6. A magical creature

7. A _____ of shoes

Down

1. I went up the

_____ way

2. You sit on it

4. You get milk at a

_____

6. Light-colored

Name _____

| stall | fall | call | small |
| tall | ball | wall | hall |

Across

3. Opposite of large

5. Made of bricks

6. A room in a house

7. To speak loudly

Down

1. Opposite of climb

2. Foot_____

3. A place where horses are kept

4. Opposite of short

Name _____

year	gear	tear	shear
fear	near	hear	appear

Across

2. To feel frightened

4. Close to

5. To cut off

8. I forgot my football _____

Down

1. Caused by crying

3. 365 days makes a _____

6. I can _____ the music

7. To be seen

our

Name _____

| pour | tourist | your | four |
| court | tournament | course | source |

Across

2. Sporting contest

5. A number

6. To tip out or _____ water

7. A tennis _____

8. It was a three-_____ meal

Down

1. The beginning

3. Traveler

4. Bring _____ own lunch

| workshop | work | word | worst |
| bookworm | worth | world | earthworm |

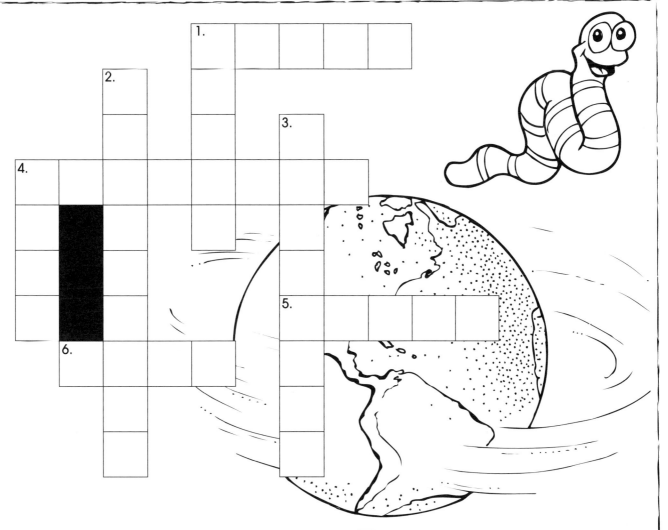

Across

1. The earth and all life
4. A place to work
5. Its value
6. Made from letters

Down

1. Very bad
2. Lives in the earth
3. A lover of books
4. A job

| wrap | wrinkle | wren | wrist |
| wrong | written | wreck | wrestle |

Across

2. Opposite of right

3. He has _____ a letter

4. Where the arm joins the hand

5. A ship_____

Down

1. A crease

2. A small bird

3. To struggle

4. To fold around

Name _____

lamb   bomb   thumb   crumb

limb   numb   comb   climb

Across

2. An arm or leg

4. A bread _____

5. It can blow up

6. Feeling no pain

Down

1. _____ your hair

2. A baby sheep

3. Part of the hand

4. To _____ a tree

k

| knee | knit | knot | knuckle |
| knew | know | knock | knife |

Across

2. I don't _____ the answer
4. Part of the hand
6. He _____ the answer
7. I can _____ a sweater

Down

1. To tie a _____
2. Part of the leg
3. Used for cutting
6. A _____ on the door

| path | past | bath | glass |
| basket | last | mast | castle |

1.

2.

3. 4.

5.

6.

Down

1. Seen on a sailboat

2. A large stone building

3. Hard and clear

4. Is filled with water

5. You walk along a

Across

4. Used to carry things

5. Opposite of first

6. The soldiers marched

_____

Name _____

| dove | glove | shovel | nothing |
| monkey | Monday | money | sponge |

Across

2. Used to buy things

5. I have _____ left

7. Soaks up water

Down

1. A small bird

2. A day of the week

3. An animal

4. Used for digging

6. Worn on your hand

World Teachers Press® www.worldteacherspress.com

| polo | open | pony | volcano |
| potato | cobra | tomato | clover |

Across

1. A vegetable
5. A sport that uses horses
7. A small horse
8. A plant

Down

2. A red fruit
3. A mountain of "fire"
4. A type of snake
6. Opposite of close

Name _____

| cent | fence | palace | celery |
| prince | cellar | cymbal | bicycle |

1.

2.

3.

4.

5. 6. 7.

8.

Across

3. Used in music

4. Part of a dollar

5. It has two wheels

8. Keeps things in or out

Down

1. Where kings or queens live

2. _____ Charming

6. A vegetable

7. Room beneath a house

World Teachers Press® www.worldteacherspress.com

face	race	place	disgrace
spice	dice	rice	twice

Across

2. A happy _____

4. Added to food for taste

6. To shame

8. Used in a boardgame

Down

1. A contest

3. Two times

5. An open space or square

7. A seed that is eaten

ge, gi

cage	rage	page	cabbage
stage	magic	giant	engine

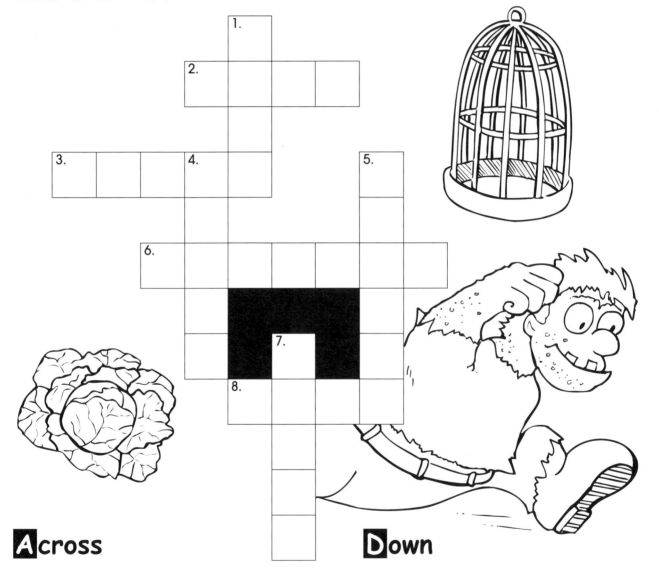

Across

2. Part of a book
3. Part of a theater
6. A vegetable
8. A bird _____

Down

1. An angry mood
4. A very large person
5. Part of a car
7. A _____ trick

Answers   Page 5

Across
2. blue
3. blunt
5. blossom
7. blind

Down
1. blink
3. blow
4. blanket
6. black

Answers   Page 6

Across
3. class
5. clever
6. clock
8. cloud

Down
1. close
2. clear
4. cluck
7. clown

Answers   Page 7

Across
1. flock
2. flounder
3. flour
5. float

Down
1. flower
2. floor
3. flash
4. flood

Answers   Page 8

Across
2. glad
3. glue
5. gleam
7. glide

Down
1. glove
3. glass
4. glare
6. globe

Answers   Page 9

Across
2. plum
3. plate
4. plenty
5. playground
6. plant

Down
1. please
4. plastic
5. planet

Answers   Page 10

Across
1. slow
2. sling
4. slipper
5. sleep

Down
1. slim
2. sleeve
5. slam

Answers   Page 11

Across
1. brave
5. bright
7. brown
8. break

Down
1. bread
2. brush
3. branch
6. breeze

Answers   Page 12

Across
2. crayon
4. creak
5. crawl
6. crab

Down
1. creek
3. cream
5. crash
6. crow

Answers   Page 13

Across
1. draw
3. dream
5. dragon
6. dress

Down
1. drag
2. drink
4. drive
6. drop

Answers   Page 14

Across
1. frog
2. frost
4. fridge
6. front

Down
1. frown
2. fresh
3. fruit
5. fried

Answers   Page 15

Across
2. grass
4. green
5. grub
7. grow

Down
1. grape
3. ground
5. growl
6. grab

Answers   Page 16

Across
2. prey
3. press
6. protect
7. price

Down
1. prize
3. pretty
4. sprint
5. present

Answers   Page 17

Across
2. trot
4. train
6. trouble
7. trick

Down
1. trunk
3. tray
4. trumpet
5. truck

Answers   Page 18

Across
2. scowl
3. screen
6. score
7. scar

Down
1. scale
3. scratch
4. escape
5. scream

Answers   Page 19

Across
2. skate
3. skirt
5. skeleton
7. skill

Down
1. skunk
3. sketch
4. skull
6. skip

Answers   Page 20

Across
1. snow
2. snap
4. sneeze
5. sniff
6. snack

Down
1. snake
3. snail
5. snatch

Answers   Page 21

Across
1. smell
2. smart
4. smooth
6. smile
7. smoke

Down
1. smash
3. small
5. smack

Answers   Page 22

Across
3. spine
5. special
6. spin

Down
1. wasp
2. speed
3. spill
4. sprint
6. sport

Answers   Page 23

Across
2. nest
4. star
5. first
7. fast

Down
1. gust
3. stick
6. start
8. step

Answers   Page 24

Across
2. swarm
3. swap
5. sweep
7. swift

Down
1. swan
2. swamp
4. sweet
6. swing

Answers   Page 25

Across
2. jump
6. melt
7. belt
8. lamp

Down
1. built
3. pump
4. stamp
5. felt

Answers   Page 26

Across
4. ant
5. tent
7. bend
8. hand

Down
1. cent
2. paint
3. friend
6. mend

Answers   Page 27

Across
2. twirl
4. tweet
7. twin
8. tweve

Down
1. twine
3. twinkle
5. twist
6. twig

Answers   Page 28

Across
1. screen
2. scrub
4. screech
5. scribble

Down
1. scrape
3. scream
4. scruffy
5. scrap

Across
2. splash
5. sprinkle
7. spray
8. spring

Down
1. splint
3. splinter
4. spread
6. split

Across
2. street
3. strong
4. strange
5. stream

Down
1. straw
2. string
3. streamer
4. stripe

Across
3. Spring
5. singing
7. ring

Down
1. fling
2. sting
3. string
4. swing
6. wing

Across
3. hunger
6. sang
7. bang

Down
1. clang
2. stung
4. rang

Across
3. crank
5. thank
6. spank
7. tank

Down
1. bank
2. drank
4. plank
6. sank

Across
1. sink
2. rink
4. twinkle
5. blink
6. pink

Down
1. shrink
3. drink
4. think

Across
2. sell
4. shell
5. fell
6. mill

Down
1. hill
2. still
3. bell
5. fill

Across
3. collar
5. full
7. dull
8. doll

Down
1. jolly
2. dollar
4. gull
6. pull

Across
2. old
4. bold
6. gold
8. cold

Down
1. fold
3. sold
5. told
7. hold

Across
2. squint
3. squeal
4. squelch
5. squirt

Down
1. squash
3. squirrel
4. squeeze
5. squid

Across
1. chick
3. cheese
4. rich

Down
1. cheer
2. chest
5. chin

Across
2. shut
4. finish
6. shoe
7. wish

Down
1. brush
3. fish
5. ship
6. shop

Across
1. thorn
2. thirteen
4. thank
5. them

Down
1. thing
2. thin
3. three
6. moth

Across
1. why
3. wheat
5. whisper
6. where

Down
1. whale
2. white
4. wheel
6. whip

Across
2. sick
4. trick
6. clock
7. black

Down
1. duck
2. sock
3. truck
5. block

Across
3. ranch
5. bunch
8. lunch

Down
1. finch
2. branch
4. punch
6. crunch
7. bench

Across
3. switch
4. match
7. hutch

Down
1. scratch
2. itch
3. stitch
5. catch
6. witch

Across
1. throat
3. thrush
4. thrill
5. through

Down
1. thrash
2. three
4. throne
5. throw

Across
3. quite
5. quack
6. question

Down
1. queer
2. quick
4. queen
5. quiet
6. quilt

Across
2. wallaby
4. wander
5. wallet
6. wash

Down
1. wasp
2. waddle
3. wattle
5. watch

Across
2. farm
5. sharp
6. shark
7. tart

Down
1. park
3. march
4. mark
5. start

Across
3. gather
4. mother
6. clever
8. fern

Down
1. father
2. jumper
5. river
7. ladder

Across
2. girl
4. skirt
5. thirst
7. bird
8. stir

Down
1. first
3. third
6. shirt

Answers — Page 52

Across
3. more
5. cork
7. thorn
8. porch

Down
1. horse
2. cork
4. born
6. torch

Answers — Page 53

Across
2. burst
6. further
8. curl

Down
1. burn
3. Saturday
4. lurch
5. turnip
7. turtle

answers — Page 54

Across
2. hay
5. tray
7. play
8. sway

Down
1. bay
3. away
4. stay
6. clay

Answers — Page 55

Across
3. parsley
4. chimney
7. donkey
8. turkey

Down
1. trolley
2. key
5. monkey
6. jockey

Answers — Page 56

Across
2. jungle
3. eagle
5. poodle
6. turtle
8. beetle

Down
1. needle
4. puddle
7. rifle

Answers — Page 57

Across
3. narrow
5. slow
6. grow
7. row
8. know

Down
1. shadow
2. hollow
4. crow

Answers — Page 58

Across
2. ahoy
3. destroy
7. boy

Down
1. joy
2. annoy
4. enjoy
5. toy
6. oyster

Answers — Page 59

Across
3. spade
4. lake
6. whale
7. cake

Down
1. plane
2. grape
3. snake
5. game

Answers — Page 60

Across
4. freeze
7. free
8. sneeze

Down
1. thirteen
2. tree
3. cheese
5. cheep
6. see

Answers — Page 61

Across
2. die
4. fried
5. tied
6. pie

Down
1. lied
2. died
3. cried
5. tie

Answers — Page 62

Across
3. hive
5. hide
7. slide

Down
1. time
2. like
4. dive
6. pipe
7. smile

Answers — Page 63

Across
1. rope
3. stone
6. throne
7. home

Down
1. rode
2. slope
4. stove
5. drove

Answers — Page 64

Across
4. rude
6. pollute
7. June

Down
1. mute
2. flute
3. salute
5. ruler
6. prune

Answers — Page 65

Across
3. goat
4. coat
5. coach
7. soak

Down
1. boat
2. float
4. croak
6. cloak

Answers — Page 66

Across
2. coin
5. moist
6. oil
8. spoil

Down
1. boil
3. noise
4. coil
7. soil

Answers — Page 67

Across
2. room
5. droop
6. boot
7. moon

Down
1. food
3. tooth
4. spoon
6. broom

Answers — Page 68

Across
2. couch
4. found
6. mouse
8. cloud

Down
1. round
3. house
5. sound
7. loud

Answers — Page 69

Across
3. mail
6. train
7. nail
8. rain

Down
1. sail
2. chain
4. stain
5. paint

Answers — Page 70

Across
2. seam
5. steam
6. sea
7. clean

Down
1. seat
3. meat
4. peach
5. speak

Answers — Page 71

Across
3. hair
5. airplane
6. fairy
7. pair

Down
1. stair
2. chair
4. dairy
6. fair

Answers — Page 72

Across
3. small
5. wall
6. hall
7. call

Down
1. fall
2. ball
3. stall
4. tall

Answers — Page 73

Across
2. fear
4. near
5. shear
8. gear

Down
1. tear
3. year
6. hear
7. appear

Answers   Page 74

Across
2. tournament
5. four
6. pour
7. court

Down
1. source
3. tourist
4. your
8. course

Answers   Page 75

Across
1. world
4. workshop
5. worth
6. word

Down
1. worst
2. earthworm
3. bookworm
4. work

Answers   Page 76

Across
2. wrong
3. written
4. wrist
5. wreck

Down
1. wrinkle
2. wren
3. wrestle
4. wrap

Answers   Page 77

Across
2. limb
4. crumb
5. bomb
6. numb

Down
1. comb
2. lamb
3. thumb
4. climb

Answers   Page 78

Across
2. know
4. knuckle
6. knew
7. knit

Down
1. knot
2. knee
3. knife
5. knock

Answers   Page 79

Across
4. basket
5. last
6. past

Down
1. mast
2. castle
3. glass
4. bath
6. path

Answers   Page 80

Across
2. money
5. nothing
7. sponge

Down
1. dove
2. Monday
3. monkey
4. shovel
6. glove

Answers   Page 81

Across
1. potato
5. polo
7. pony
8. clover

Down
2. tomato
3. volcano
4. cobra
6. open

Answers   Page 82

Across
3. cymbal
4. cent
5. bicycle
8. fence

Down
1. palace
2. prince
6. celery
7. cellar

Answers   Page 83

Across
2. face
4. spice
6. disgrace
8. dice

Down
1. race
3. twice
5. place
7. rice

Answers   Page 84

Across
2. page
3. stage
6. cabbage
8. cage

Down
1. rage
4. giant
5. engine
7. magic